THE BUSINESS SUCCESS GUIDE TO CHICKEN FARMING

Comprehensive Insight To Raising Healthy Fowl, Organic Egg Production, Sustainable Practices, And Profitable Poultry Management

RICHMOND HAMILL

© 2024 [RICHMOND HAMILL]. All rights reserved.

Except for brief quotations included in critical reviews and certain other noncommercial uses allowed by copyright law, no part of this book may be reproduced, distributed, or transmitted in any form or by any means, including photocopying, recording, or other electronic or mechanical methods, without the publisher's prior written permission.

Disclaimer

The information presented in this book is based on the author's personal knowledge and understanding of livestock management. The author is not affiliated with any association, company, business, or individual in the livestock industry. All content is provided for informational purposes only and should not be considered as professional advice. Readers are encouraged to seek professional guidance and conduct their own research before making any decisions based on the information contained in this book. The author and publisher disclaim any liability for any adverse effects or consequences resulting from the use of the information contained herein.

Table of Contents

CHAPTER ONE 17

Introduction To Chicken Farming 17

Overview Of Chicken Farming 17

Benefits Of Raising Chickens 18

Types Of Chickens And Their Uses 20

- Egg Layers: 20
- Meat Birds (Broilers): 20
- Dual-Purpose Breeds: 21

Basic Terminology And Concepts 21

- Brooder: 21
- Coop: 21
- Roost: 22
- Layer Feed: 22
- Grit: 22
- Molting: 22

Getting Started: What You'll Need 22

1. Chicken Coop: 23
2. Chicken Run: 23
3. Feed and Water: 23
4. Brooder: 23
5. Nesting Boxes: 24
6. Grit and Oyster Shell: 24
7. Health Supplies: 24

CHAPTER TWO 25

Setting Up Your Chicken Farm 25

Choosing The Right Location 25

1. Climate and Weather: 25
2. Accessibility: 26
3. Water Supply: 26
4. Soil Quality and Drainage: 26

Designing The Coop And Run 27

1. Coop Design: 27
2. Nesting Boxes and Perches: 28
3. Chicken Run: 28
4. Bedding and Maintenance: 29

Essential Equipment And Supplies 29

1. Feeders and Waterers: 29
2. Heating and Lighting: 30
3. Health and Safety Supplies: 30
4. Nesting Materials: 30

Understanding Local Regulations 31

1. Zoning Laws: 31
2. Permits and Licenses: 31
3. Animal Welfare Standards: 32
4. Biosecurity Measures: 32

Budgeting And Planning For Start-Up Costs ... 33

1. Initial Investment: 33

2. Operating Costs: 33

3. Revenue Projections: 34

4. Financial Planning: 34

CHAPTER THREE 35

Selecting The Right Breeds 35

Common Chicken Breeds And Their Traits 35

Choosing Breeds For Meat Vs. Eggs 36

Considerations For Climate And Space 37

Buying Chicks Vs. Mature Birds 38

Evaluating Breed Performance And Needs 39

CHAPTER FOUR 41

Housing And Environment 41

Building A Safe And Comfortable Coop 41

Ensuring Proper Ventilation And Lighting 43

Providing Space For Roaming And Foraging .. 44

Maintaining Cleanliness And Hygiene 46

Managing Temperature And Weather Conditions..47

CHAPTER FIVE 49

Feeding And Nutrition 49

Basics Of Chicken Nutrition...........................49

Selecting The Right Feed For Different Ages ..50

Supplementing With Scraps And Treats 52

Understanding Water Needs And Hydration ..53

Avoiding Common Feeding Mistakes 54

CHAPTER SIX 57

Health And Care 57

Recognizing Signs Of Illness 57

Vaccinations And Preventative Measures.......58

Parasite Control And Management 60

Daily Care Routine 61

Emergency First Aid For Chickens 62

CHAPTER SEVEN 65

Breeding And Incubation 65

Understanding Chicken Reproduction 65

Setting Up For Incubation 66

Incubation Techniques And Equipment 68

Caring For Chicks After Hatching 69

Managing Breeding Programs 71

CHAPTER EIGHT 73

Egg Production And Management 73

Collecting And Storing Eggs 73

    Proper Egg Collection Techniques 73

    Storing Eggs Correctly 73

    Cleaning Eggs 74

Managing Egg Quality And Size 75

    Factors Affecting Egg Quality 75

    Controlling Egg Size 75

    Handling and Sorting Eggs 76

Understanding Egg Laying Cycles 76

Natural Egg Laying Cycles 76

Managing Light Exposure 77

Molting and Egg Production 77

Troubleshooting Egg Production Issues 78

Common Production Problems 78

Disease and Parasite Control 79

Environmental Adjustments 79

Marketing And Selling Eggs 80

Creating a Marketing Plan 80

Packaging and Presentation 80

Pricing and Distribution 81

CHAPTER NINE 83

Harvesting And Processing Meat 83

Best Practices For Slaughtering Chickens 83

Processing And Butchering Techniques 84

Storing And Preserving Meat 86

Ensuring Meat Quality And Safety 87

Marketing And Selling Poultry Products 88

CHAPTER TEN 91

Troubleshooting And Problem-Solving 91

Common Problems And Solutions 91

Dealing With Predators And Pests 93

Managing Unexpected Expenses 94

Handling Behavioral Issues 96

Resources For Further Help And Information 97

Frequently Ask Questions And Answers 99

CONCLUSION 106

THE END 110

ABOUT THIS BOOK

"Chicken Farming" is an essential guide for anyone interested in venturing into poultry farming, whether as a hobbyist or a commercial farmer. This comprehensive book provides a detailed introduction to chicken farming, highlighting the numerous benefits of raising chickens, such as a sustainable source of eggs and meat, natural pest control, and the joy of keeping these engaging animals. It outlines the different types of chickens and their various uses, ensuring that readers can make informed decisions about the best breeds for their specific needs. This book also covers the fundamental terminology and concepts of chicken farming, making it accessible for beginners.

Setting up a chicken farm requires careful planning, and this book meticulously guides readers through the process of choosing the right location, designing an efficient coop and run, and gathering essential equipment and supplies. It emphasizes the importance of understanding local regulations to ensure compliance and avoid potential legal issues. Additionally, this book provides valuable insights into budgeting and planning for start-up costs, helping readers establish a financially viable farming operation.

Selecting the right breeds is crucial for a successful chicken farming venture. This book offers an in-depth look at common chicken breeds and their traits, providing guidance on choosing breeds for meat versus egg production, and considering factors such as climate and available space. It also discusses the pros and cons of buying chicks versus mature birds and offers advice on evaluating breed performance and needs to ensure the best results for the farm.

Proper housing and environment are key to the well-being of chickens. This book details the construction of a safe and comfortable coop, the importance of ventilation and lighting, and the provision of adequate space for roaming and foraging. It underscores the necessity of maintaining cleanliness and hygiene to prevent diseases and manage temperature and weather conditions effectively.

Feeding and nutrition are covered comprehensively, with information on the basics of chicken nutrition, selecting appropriate feed for different ages, and supplementing diets with scraps and treats. This book highlights the importance of understanding water needs and hydration, as well as avoiding common feeding mistakes that can affect the health and productivity of the flock.

Health and care are paramount in chicken farming. This book teaches readers how to recognize signs of illness, implement vaccinations and preventative measures, and control parasites. It outlines a daily care routine and provides emergency first aid tips, ensuring that farmers are well-prepared to handle any health issues that may arise.

Breeding and incubation are also thoroughly explored, with sections on chicken reproduction, setting up for incubation, and using incubation techniques and equipment. This book guides readers through the care of chicks after hatching and the management of breeding programs, which are essential for maintaining a productive flock.

Egg production and management are crucial for those focusing on egg-laying chickens. This book offers practical advice on collecting and storing eggs, managing egg quality and size, understanding egg-laying cycles, and troubleshooting production issues. It also covers the marketing and selling of eggs, providing strategies for maximizing profitability.

For those interested in meat production, This book details best practices for slaughtering chickens, processing and butchering techniques, and storing and preserving meat. It emphasizes ensuring meat quality and safety and offers tips for marketing and selling poultry products.

Finally, This book addresses troubleshooting and problem-solving, with sections on common problems and solutions, dealing with predators and pests, managing unexpected expenses, and handling behavioral issues. It also provides resources for further help and information, ensuring that readers have access to the support they need to succeed in their chicken farming endeavors.

CHAPTER ONE

Introduction To Chicken Farming

Overview Of Chicken Farming

Chicken farming is the practice of raising domesticated chickens to obtain meat, eggs, or both. This can be done on a small scale in a backyard or on a larger scale in a commercial farm. The practice has been around for thousands of years and continues to be a popular and sustainable way to produce food. Chicken farming can provide a reliable source of income and self-sufficiency for many people.

The primary goal of chicken farming is to create a healthy environment where chickens can thrive and produce high-quality eggs or meat. This involves proper housing, feeding, and healthcare. A well-managed chicken farm can be both profitable and rewarding, offering fresh products for personal consumption or sale. The initial investment can vary, but the returns, in terms of food security and financial gain, can be substantial.

Starting a chicken farm requires careful planning and consideration of various factors, such as the type of chickens you want to raise, the space available, and the resources needed. By understanding the basics of chicken farming, beginners can make informed decisions and set up a successful operation.

Benefits Of Raising Chickens

Raising chickens offers numerous benefits, both practical and personal. One of the most significant advantages is the production of fresh eggs. Backyard chickens can lay a steady supply of eggs, which are fresher and often tastier than store-bought alternatives.

Additionally, raising chickens for meat can provide a sustainable and humane source of protein.

Another benefit of chicken farming is the role chickens play in pest control. Chickens naturally forage for insects, which helps to keep the pest population in check. This can reduce the need for chemical pesticides in your garden or farm. Furthermore, chickens produce valuable manure that can be used as a natural fertilizer, enhancing soil fertility and promoting healthy plant growth.

Raising chickens can also be a fulfilling and educational experience. It provides an opportunity to learn about animal husbandry, responsibility, and the cycle of life. Chickens can be a source of companionship and enjoyment, and they offer a way to connect with nature and the environment. For families, it can be a great way to teach children about where their food comes from and the importance of caring for animals.

Types Of Chickens And Their Uses

Chickens can be broadly categorized into three main types: egg layers, meat birds (broilers), and dual-purpose breeds. Each type has specific characteristics and is bred for different purposes.

Egg Layers: These chickens are bred primarily for their egg-laying capabilities. Popular egg-laying breeds include Leghorns, Rhode Island Reds, and Sussex. These birds are known for their high egg production and consistent laying. They are typically lighter in weight and have a more active disposition compared to meat birds.

Meat Birds (Broilers): Meat birds are bred specifically for rapid growth and meat production. The most common breed is the Cornish Cross, which is known for its fast growth rate and high meat yield. These birds are usually processed at a young age, around 6-8 weeks, to ensure tender meat.

Dual-Purpose Breeds: Dual-purpose breeds are versatile chickens that can be raised for both eggs and meat. Examples include the Plymouth Rock, Orpington, and Wyandotte. These birds offer a balance between egg production and meat quality, making them a good choice for small-scale farmers who want the benefits of both.

Basic Terminology And Concepts

To successfully navigate chicken farming, it's important to understand some basic terminology and concepts:

Brooder: A heated area or device used to raise young chicks until they can regulate their body temperature.

Coop: The housing structure where chickens live. It provides shelter and protection from predators.

Run An enclosed outdoor area attached to the coop where chickens can exercise and forage.

Roost: A perch where chickens sleep at night. It should be elevated and comfortable for the birds.

Layer Feed: Specialized feed formulated to meet the nutritional needs of egg-laying hens.

Grit: Small stones or sand that chickens consume to aid in digestion. It helps grind food in their gizzard.

Molting: The process where chickens shed old feathers and grow new ones. It typically occurs annually and can affect egg production.

Getting Started: What You'll Need

To start chicken farming, you'll need to gather some essential supplies and prepare your space. Here are the key items and steps to get started:

1. **Chicken Coop:** Purchase or build a sturdy chicken coop that provides adequate space, ventilation, and protection from predators. The coop should have nesting boxes for egg-laying and roosting bars for sleeping.

2. **Chicken Run:** Create a secure outdoor run attached to the coop where chickens can roam and forage. The run should be predator-proof with fencing and a covered top to prevent aerial attacks.

3. **Feed and Water:** Provide high-quality feed appropriate for the type of chickens you are raising. Layer feed for egg layers, broiler feed for meat birds, or a balanced feed for dual-purpose breeds. Ensure a constant supply of clean, fresh water.

4. **Brooder:** If starting with chicks, set up a brooder with a heat lamp, bedding, and chick starter feed. Maintain the appropriate temperature and gradually reduce heat as the chicks grow.

5. **Nesting Boxes:** Install nesting boxes in the coop for egg-laying hens. Each box should be filled with clean bedding and offer privacy for the hens.

6. **Grit and Oyster Shell:** Provide grit for digestion and oyster shell for calcium supplementation, especially for laying hens.

7. **Health Supplies:** Keep basic health supplies on hand, such as poultry vitamins, electrolytes, and first aid items. Monitor your flock regularly for signs of illness and address issues promptly.

By gathering these supplies and setting up your space, you'll be well-prepared to start your chicken farming journey. With proper care and management, your chickens will thrive and provide you with fresh eggs and meat.

CHAPTER TWO

Setting Up Your Chicken Farm

Choosing The Right Location

Selecting the right location for your chicken farm is crucial for the success and sustainability of your poultry venture. A good location should provide a conducive environment for the chickens, ensure their safety, and allow for efficient farm operations. Here are the key considerations:

1. **Climate and Weather:** Chickens are sensitive to extreme weather conditions. Choose a location with a moderate climate, where temperatures do not fluctuate drastically. Consider the availability of shade in hotter climates and protection from wind and rain in cooler regions. This will ensure the well-being of your chickens throughout the year.

2.   **Accessibility:** Your farm should be easily accessible by road for the transportation of supplies, feed, and the movement of chickens. Proximity to markets is also important to facilitate the sale of eggs and meat. An accessible location will reduce transportation costs and make farm management more convenient.

3.   **Water Supply:** A reliable source of clean water is essential for chicken farming. Chickens need a consistent supply of fresh water for drinking and maintaining hygiene. Ensure that your chosen location has access to a clean and abundant water supply to meet the daily needs of your flock.

4.   **Soil Quality and Drainage:** The soil quality and drainage of the location should be assessed. Good drainage is necessary to prevent waterlogging, which can lead to muddy conditions and increase the risk of diseases. Additionally, the soil should be able to support the growth of vegetation in the chicken

run area, providing natural foraging opportunities for the birds.

Designing The Coop And Run

The design of the coop and run is a critical aspect of chicken farming, impacting the health, productivity, and safety of your flock. Here's how to design them effectively:

1. Coop Design: The coop should provide a safe and comfortable shelter for the chickens. It should be well-ventilated to ensure fresh air circulation while protecting the birds from drafts. The coop should also be predator-proof, with sturdy construction and secure locks on doors and windows. Adequate space is essential; a general rule is to allow at least 2-3 square feet per chicken inside the coop.

2. **Nesting Boxes and Perches:** Nesting boxes are essential for laying hens, providing a quiet and private space for egg-laying. Each box should be about 12x12 inches and filled with soft bedding material. Perches or roosting bars should be installed inside the coop, allowing chickens to roost off the ground at night. This mimics their natural behavior and helps keep them safe from ground-dwelling predators.

3. **Chicken Run:** The chicken run is an outdoor space where chickens can roam, forage, and exercise. The run should be enclosed with a sturdy fence to protect against predators and prevent the chickens from wandering off. Ensure there is enough space for the chickens to move freely; about 8-10 square feet per chicken is recommended. The run should also include shaded areas to protect the chickens from the sun.

4. **Bedding and Maintenance:** The coop and run should be kept clean and dry to prevent the buildup of ammonia from chicken waste. Use absorbent bedding material such as straw, wood shavings, or sand in the coop and nesting boxes. Regularly clean and replace bedding to maintain a healthy environment. Consider using the deep litter method, where bedding is periodically turned over and added to, creating compost over time.

Essential Equipment And Supplies

Equipping your chicken farm with the right tools and supplies is vital for efficient management and the well-being of your flock. Here are the essentials:

1. **Feeders and Waterers:** Invest in durable and easy-to-clean feeders and waterers. Automatic or gravity-fed systems can save time and ensure a constant supply of food and water.

Place them at an appropriate height to prevent contamination from droppings.

2. **Heating and Lighting:** If you live in a region with cold winters, consider installing a heat source in the coop to keep the chickens warm. Use safe, poultry-approved heating lamps or pads. Additionally, artificial lighting can help maintain egg production during shorter days in winter.

3. **Health and Safety Supplies:** Keep a stock of basic health supplies such as first aid kits, medications, and vitamins. Regularly check for signs of illness and provide necessary treatments promptly. Ensure you have equipment for cleaning and disinfecting the coop and run to maintain hygiene.

4. **Nesting Materials:** Stock up on nesting materials like straw or wood shavings to keep the nesting boxes clean and comfortable for laying hens.

Regularly replace the nesting material to ensure a fresh environment for egg-laying.

Understanding Local Regulations

Complying with local regulations is essential to avoid legal issues and ensure the smooth operation of your chicken farm. Here's how to navigate the regulatory landscape:

1. **Zoning Laws:** Check local zoning laws to ensure that your property is zoned for agricultural use. Some areas have restrictions on keeping livestock, including chickens, so it's important to verify that your farm complies with these regulations.

2. **Permits and Licenses:** Obtain any necessary permits and licenses required for operating a chicken farm. This may include permits for building the coop, running a commercial farm, or selling eggs and

meat. Contact your local agricultural or municipal office for specific requirements.

3. **Animal Welfare Standards:** Familiarize yourself with animal welfare standards and regulations to ensure the humane treatment of your chickens. This includes providing adequate space, nutrition, and veterinary care. Compliance with these standards is not only ethical but also beneficial for the health and productivity of your flock.

4. **Biosecurity Measures:** Implement biosecurity measures to prevent the spread of diseases on your farm. This includes controlling the movement of people and equipment, regular cleaning and disinfection, and proper disposal of waste. Understanding and adhering to biosecurity guidelines will help protect your flock from infections.

Budgeting And Planning For Start-Up Costs

Effective budgeting and planning are crucial for the successful establishment of your chicken farm. Here's how to manage your finances:

1. **Initial Investment:** Calculate the initial investment required for setting up your farm. This includes the cost of land, building the coop and run, purchasing equipment and supplies, and acquiring the first batch of chickens. Ensure you have a clear understanding of all expenses to avoid unexpected costs.

2. **Operating Costs:** Estimate the ongoing operating costs such as feed, bedding, healthcare, utilities, and maintenance. Include costs for marketing and transportation if you plan to sell eggs or meat.

Creating a detailed budget will help you manage your expenses and ensure the financial viability of your farm.

3. **Revenue Projections:** Develop revenue projections based on the expected production of eggs or meat. Consider factors such as market demand, pricing, and potential sales channels. This will help you gauge the profitability of your farm and make informed decisions.

4. **Financial Planning:** Explore funding options such as loans, grants, or investments to support your start-up costs. Create a financial plan that outlines your funding sources, repayment schedules, and strategies for managing cash flow. Proper financial planning will ensure you have the resources needed to sustain and grow your chicken farm.

CHAPTER THREE

Selecting The Right Breeds

Common Chicken Breeds And Their Traits

Choosing the right chicken breed is crucial for a successful farming venture. There are numerous breeds, each with unique characteristics that suit different farming objectives. Some of the most common breeds include the Rhode Island Red, Leghorn, Sussex, and Plymouth Rock.

The Rhode Island Red is known for its hardiness and ability to lay a significant number of brown eggs, making it a popular choice for egg production. These birds are also good foragers and adapt well to free-range conditions. On the other hand, Leghorns are prolific white egg layers and are favored for commercial egg production due to their efficiency and high productivity. They are, however, less hardy than Rhode Island Reds and may require more care in colder climates.

Sussex chickens are dual-purpose birds, suitable for both meat and egg production. They have a calm temperament and are excellent for beginners. Plymouth Rock chickens are another dual-purpose breed, known for their pleasant nature and steady egg production. They are robust and can thrive in various environments, making them a versatile option for many farmers.

Choosing Breeds For Meat Vs. Eggs

When selecting breeds, it's essential to decide whether your primary goal is meat production, egg production, or a combination of both. Meat-specific breeds, like Cornish Cross and Jersey Giant, are bred to grow quickly and produce tender, high-quality meat. Cornish Cross chickens, for instance, reach market weight in as little as six to eight weeks, making them ideal for rapid turnover in meat production.

For egg production, breeds like the aforementioned Rhode Island Red, Leghorn, and Australorp are top choices. These breeds are known for their high egg-laying capacity, with some laying up to 300 eggs per year. If you want both meat and eggs, dual-purpose breeds like Sussex, Plymouth Rock, and Orpington are ideal. They provide a steady supply of eggs and grow to a good size for meat production, offering flexibility for small-scale farmers.

Considerations For Climate And Space

The climate of your region significantly impacts which breeds will thrive on your farm. Cold-hardy breeds, such as the Wyandotte and Buff Orpington, have dense feathers and can withstand harsh winters. These breeds are well-suited for regions with cold climates, ensuring your flock remains healthy and productive throughout the year.

In warmer climates, heat-tolerant breeds like the Leghorn and Andalusian are better choices. These birds have lighter feathers and can handle high temperatures more effectively. Additionally, adequate space is crucial for the well-being of your chickens. Breeds that are more active and require more space include the Rhode Island Red and Sussex. If you have limited space, bantam breeds or more docile chickens like the Cochin can be a good fit.

Buying Chicks Vs. Mature Birds

When starting your chicken farm, you can choose to buy either chicks or mature birds. Buying chicks is more cost-effective and allows you to raise them in your environment, ensuring they adapt well to your farm. However, chicks require more care, including brooding, feeding, and vaccination. They are more vulnerable to disease and environmental stressors, so beginners need to be prepared for intensive initial care.

Mature birds, or pullets, are already past the vulnerable chick stage and closer to their productive period. This option is more expensive but reduces the risk and time associated with raising chicks. For beginners, starting with a few mature birds can simplify the process, allowing you to focus on learning the basics of chicken farming without the added challenge of raising chicks.

Evaluating Breed Performance And Needs

Regularly evaluating the performance and needs of your chosen breeds is crucial for maintaining a productive and healthy flock.

Monitor egg production rates, growth rates, and overall health to ensure your chickens are thriving. Keep detailed records of each breed's performance to identify any issues early and adjust your management practices accordingly.

Nutrition, housing, and healthcare are critical factors influencing breed performance. Ensure your chickens receive a balanced diet rich in protein, vitamins, and minerals. Provide clean and spacious housing to prevent stress and disease. Regular health checks and vaccinations are essential to keep your flock healthy.

By carefully selecting breeds that match your farming goals, climate, and space, and by continually evaluating their performance, you can create a successful and sustainable chicken farming operation.

CHAPTER FOUR

Housing And Environment

Building A Safe And Comfortable Coop

Creating a safe and comfortable coop for your chickens is the foundation of successful chicken farming. Begin by selecting a suitable location that is elevated to prevent waterlogging and flooding. The coop should be constructed using durable materials such as treated wood or metal to withstand various weather conditions. Ensure the coop has a solid floor, which can be made of concrete or compacted dirt covered with bedding materials like straw or wood shavings. This setup not only provides comfort but also helps in maintaining cleanliness.

The coop should be predator-proof to protect your chickens from animals like raccoons, foxes, and dogs.

Use hardware cloth instead of chicken wire for fencing, as it is stronger and provides better protection. Secure all openings, including windows and doors, with locks to prevent predators from gaining access. Additionally, consider burying the fencing at least 12 inches underground to deter digging predators.

Inside the coop, create nesting boxes and perches. Nesting boxes should be placed in a quiet, dark area to encourage hens to lay eggs. Each box should be approximately 12x12 inches, lined with soft bedding, and easily accessible. Perches should be positioned higher than the nesting boxes to mimic natural roosting behavior. Provide enough space to allow each chicken to perch comfortably without overcrowding.

Ensuring Proper Ventilation And Lighting

Proper ventilation and lighting are crucial for the health and productivity of your chickens. Ventilation helps remove moisture, ammonia, and other harmful gases from the coop, reducing the risk of respiratory problems. Install vents near the roof to allow hot air to escape while preventing drafts at the chicken's level. Windows and doors can also be used for ventilation, but they should be covered with hardware cloth to keep out predators and pests.

Lighting plays a significant role in egg production and overall chicken well-being. Chickens need about 14-16 hours of light per day to maintain consistent egg laying. In the winter months, when daylight hours are shorter, supplement natural light with artificial lighting. Use a timer to ensure the lights turn on and off at the same time each day, maintaining a consistent light schedule. Avoid using harsh lighting; instead, opt for soft, warm lights that mimic natural sunlight.

To maximize ventilation and lighting, keep the coop clean and clutter-free. Regularly remove dust and cobwebs from vents and light fixtures to maintain optimal airflow and light distribution. Position the coop in an area that receives ample natural light but also has some shade to protect the chickens from extreme heat.

Providing Space For Roaming And Foraging

Chickens thrive when they have enough space to roam and forage. An overcrowded coop can lead to stress, aggressive behavior, and health issues. The general rule of thumb is to provide at least 4 square feet of indoor space and 10 square feet of outdoor space per chicken. This allows them to move freely, exercise, and exhibit natural behaviors.

Create an outdoor run attached to the coop where chickens can scratch the ground, hunt for insects, and enjoy fresh air and sunlight. Secure the run with sturdy fencing and a cover to protect against predators and aerial threats like hawks. Consider using a portable run or chicken tractor that can be moved to different areas of your yard, providing fresh grazing opportunities and reducing the risk of overgrazing in one spot.

In addition to the run, provide enrichment activities to keep your chickens entertained and stimulated. Scatter feed or scratch grains in the run to encourage foraging. Install dust baths filled with fine sand or diatomaceous earth, where chickens can clean themselves and control parasites. Add perches, logs, and other structures to create a dynamic environment that promotes physical and mental well-being.

Maintaining Cleanliness And Hygiene

Maintaining cleanliness and hygiene in the coop is essential for preventing disease and promoting the health of your flock. Start by implementing a regular cleaning schedule. Remove soiled bedding, droppings, and uneaten food daily. Every week, conduct a thorough cleaning by removing all bedding, scrubbing surfaces with a mild disinfectant, and allowing the coop to dry completely before adding fresh bedding.

Ensure that feeding and watering systems are kept clean and sanitary. Use feeders and waterers that are easy to clean and refill. Clean these containers regularly to prevent the growth of mold, algae, and bacteria. Place them at a height that prevents chickens from scratching bedding or dirt into them but still allows easy access.

Manage waste effectively by using the deep litter method or composting. The deep litter method involves adding fresh bedding on top of old bedding, allowing it to decompose gradually and generate heat, which can help keep the coop warm in colder months. Periodically turn the bedding to aid decomposition and control odor. Alternatively, collect chicken waste and bedding in a compost bin, turning it regularly to produce rich compost that can be used in your garden.

Managing Temperature And Weather Conditions

Managing temperature and weather conditions is crucial to keep your chickens comfortable and healthy throughout the year. Chickens are hardy animals, but extreme temperatures can stress them and affect their productivity. In hot weather, provide ample shade and ensure the coop has proper ventilation to prevent overheating. Place waterers in shaded areas and add ice to the water to keep it cool. Consider using fans or misters to reduce heat stress.

In cold weather, insulate the coop to retain heat and prevent drafts. Use materials like straw bales or foam boards to insulate walls and the roof. Provide a heat source, such as a heat lamp or radiant heater, but ensure it is safe and does not pose a fire hazard. Increase bedding depth to help chickens generate warmth and maintain a comfortable temperature inside the coop.

Monitor weather conditions and take appropriate measures to protect your chickens. During heavy rains, ensure the coop and run are well-drained to prevent flooding. In snowy conditions, clear snow from the coop entrance and pathways to allow chickens to move freely.

CHAPTER FIVE

Feeding And Nutrition

Basics Of Chicken Nutrition

Understanding the fundamentals of chicken nutrition is crucial for maintaining a healthy and productive flock. Chickens, like all animals, require a balanced diet that includes proteins, carbohydrates, fats, vitamins, and minerals. Protein is essential for growth, feather development, and egg production. Typically, a layer feed will contain about 16-18% protein, whereas broiler feed may contain up to 22% to support rapid growth.

Carbohydrates provide the energy chickens need for their daily activities, including foraging and egg-laying. Common sources include grains like corn, wheat, and barley.

Fats, while needed in smaller quantities, are vital for energy storage and the absorption of fat-soluble vitamins (A, D, E, and K).

Vitamins and minerals, though required in minute amounts, play critical roles in various physiological functions. For instance, calcium is necessary for strong eggshells, while phosphorus supports skeletal health. Ensuring that chickens receive a diet balanced in these nutrients is fundamental to their overall health and productivity.

Selecting The Right Feed For Different Ages

Different stages of a chicken's life require specific nutritional needs, and selecting the appropriate feed is essential. Chick starter feed is designed for chicks up to eight weeks old and typically contains 18-20% protein to support their rapid growth and development.

It's crucial to provide starter feed in a form that chicks can easily consume, such as crumbles.

From eight weeks to around 18 weeks, pullets (young hens) should be transitioned to a grower feed, which contains slightly less protein (16-18%) and balanced levels of vitamins and minerals to support steady growth without causing excessive weight gain.

Once hens begin laying eggs, they should be fed a layer feed, which contains about 16% protein and higher levels of calcium to support eggshell production. It's essential to provide layer feed once the first egg is laid to ensure the hens have the necessary nutrients for consistent and healthy egg production.

Supplementing With Scraps And Treats

While commercial feed should be the primary source of nutrition, supplementing with kitchen scraps and treats can provide variety and additional nutrients. Scraps such as vegetable peels, fruit scraps, and whole grains can be offered in moderation. Protein-rich treats like mealworms, cooked eggs, and yogurt can also be beneficial, especially during molting periods when protein needs are higher.

It's important to avoid feeding chickens scraps that are harmful to their health, such as chocolate, caffeine, raw potato peels, and anything moldy or spoiled. Introducing new treats slowly and observing the chickens' reactions can help ensure their diet remains balanced and doesn't lead to digestive issues or nutrient deficiencies.

Understanding Water Needs And Hydration

Adequate hydration is as crucial as proper nutrition. Chickens require a constant supply of clean, fresh water. On average, a chicken will drink about half a liter of water per day, though this can increase significantly in hot weather or during periods of high egg production.

Water should be provided in containers that are easy for chickens to access but difficult to contaminate. Hanging waterers or nipple water systems can help keep the water clean. In colder climates, it's important to ensure the water doesn't freeze, which may require heated water or frequent checks to replace frozen water.

Electrolytes and vitamins can be added to the water occasionally to support hydration and overall health, especially during periods of stress, illness, or extreme temperatures.

Avoiding Common Feeding Mistakes

Several common feeding mistakes can negatively impact the health and productivity of your flock. Overfeeding or underfeeding is a major issue. It's essential to follow feeding guidelines based on the type and age of the chickens to ensure they receive the correct amount of nutrients without causing obesity or malnutrition.

Another common mistake is offering too many treats, which can dilute the nutritional balance of their diet and lead to deficiencies. Treats should not make up more than 10% of the total diet.

Improper storage of feed can also lead to issues such as mold growth or nutrient degradation.

The feed should be stored in a cool, dry place, preferably in sealed containers to protect it from moisture and pests.

Finally, neglecting to provide grit can affect digestion. Chickens need grit (small stones or commercial grit) to help grind up their food in the gizzard, especially if they consume whole grains or foraged food.

By understanding and implementing these feeding and nutrition principles, you can ensure your chickens are healthy, productive, and well-cared for.

CHAPTER SIX

Health And Care

Recognizing Signs Of Illness

Recognizing signs of illness in chickens is crucial for maintaining a healthy flock. Observing your birds daily helps in identifying any abnormalities early. Common signs of illness include lethargy, reduced appetite, abnormal droppings, and changes in comb color. Chickens may also exhibit respiratory symptoms such as coughing, sneezing, or nasal discharge. Behavioral changes, like hiding or isolation, can also indicate health issues.

Physical examination is key. Check for any signs of external parasites such as lice or mites. Look for any unusual lumps, wounds, or swellings on the body. Eyes should be clear and bright; any cloudiness or discharge is a red flag.

Additionally, listen for any abnormal sounds, like wheezing or labored breathing, which could suggest respiratory problems.

If you suspect a chicken is ill, isolate it from the rest of the flock to prevent the potential spread of disease. Keep detailed records of symptoms and any treatments administered. This can be helpful for a veterinarian if professional intervention is needed. Promptly addressing health issues ensures the well-being of your entire flock.

Vaccinations And Preventative Measures

Vaccinations are an essential part of chicken health management. They help protect against common poultry diseases such as Marek's disease, Newcastle disease, and infectious bronchitis. Many hatcheries vaccinate chicks before they are sold, but additional vaccinations may be necessary as the birds grow.

Consult with a veterinarian to develop a vaccination schedule tailored to your flock's needs.

Preventative measures go beyond vaccinations. Maintaining a clean coop and living environment reduces the risk of disease. Regularly remove droppings and replace bedding to minimize exposure to harmful bacteria. Ensure proper ventilation in the coop to reduce moisture buildup, which can promote the growth of pathogens.

Quarantine new birds before introducing them to your existing flock. This helps prevent the introduction of diseases. Provide a balanced diet with essential nutrients to boost the chickens' immune systems. Clean waterers and feeders regularly to avoid contamination. Practicing good biosecurity measures, such as limiting visitors to your coop and wearing clean clothing when handling birds, further reduces disease risk.

Parasite Control And Management

Parasite control is vital for the health and productivity of your chickens. External parasites, such as mites and lice, can cause discomfort and lead to more serious health issues. Regularly inspect your chickens for signs of parasites, including feather loss, scabs, and restless behavior. Treat infestations promptly with appropriate insecticides, ensuring you follow the manufacturer's instructions.

Internal parasites, such as worms, can also pose significant health risks. Routine deworming is recommended, especially if you notice symptoms like weight loss, diarrhea, or lethargy. Use a deworming medication specifically designed for poultry and follow a schedule advised by a veterinarian.

Maintaining a clean environment is crucial for parasite control. Regularly clean and disinfect the coop, paying special attention to nesting boxes and roosting areas. Provide dust baths for your chickens, as they naturally help control external parasites. Adding diatomaceous earth to dust baths can enhance their effectiveness.

Daily Care Routine

Establishing a daily care routine is essential for maintaining a healthy and happy flock. Begin each day by checking on your chickens. Observe their behavior and appearance to catch any signs of illness early. Ensure they have access to clean, fresh water and replenish it as needed. Provide a balanced feed appropriate for their age and purpose, whether they are layers, broilers, or dual-purpose birds.

Collect eggs daily to keep the nesting boxes clean and to encourage hens to lay in designated areas.

Remove any droppings and replace soiled bedding to maintain a clean environment. Regularly check and clean feeders and waterers to prevent contamination.

Spend time interacting with your chickens to build trust and make them easier to handle. Handle them gently to inspect for any signs of injury or illness. Ensure they have access to dust baths, which help them manage external parasites and keep their feathers in good condition.

Emergency First Aid For Chickens

Knowing how to administer emergency first aid can save a chicken's life. Have a first aid kit on hand with essential items such as wound disinfectant, bandages, scissors, tweezers, and a small flashlight. In case of minor cuts or wounds, clean the area thoroughly with a disinfectant and apply an appropriate wound treatment.

Use gauze and bandages to protect the wound and prevent further injury or infection.

For broken bones, immobilize the affected area with a splint and secure it with bandages. Ensure the chicken is kept quiet and separate from the flock to minimize movement while it heals. For heat stress, move the chicken to a cooler area immediately and offer cool water. You can also use a damp cloth to gently lower its body temperature.

In cases of severe illness or injury, consult a veterinarian promptly. Keep the affected chicken isolated from the flock to prevent the spread of disease. Maintaining a detailed log of symptoms and treatments administered can be invaluable for ongoing care and veterinary consultation. Being prepared and knowledgeable about first aid ensures you can provide immediate and effective care in emergencies.

CHAPTER SEVEN

Breeding And Incubation

Understanding Chicken Reproduction

Chicken reproduction involves a detailed understanding of their mating habits, egg production, and fertilization. Hens typically reach maturity and start laying eggs at about 18 to 20 weeks of age. Roosters, on the other hand, become sexually mature slightly earlier. In a typical mating process, the rooster mounts the hen and transfers sperm, which then travels to the hen's oviduct to fertilize the eggs.

The process of egg formation begins with ovulation, where the hen's ovary releases an ovum (yolk). This travels down the oviduct, where it encounters sperm if mating has occurred.

Fertilization takes place, and the yolk continues its journey, gathering layers of albumen (egg white), membranes, and eventually a shell. This entire process takes about 24 to 26 hours, and hens can lay eggs almost daily, whether fertilized or not.

To ensure fertilized eggs, a typical ratio is one rooster for every 10 to 12 hens. This balance maximizes the chances of successful mating while preventing the hens from being over-mated, which can cause stress and injury. Observing the flock can help determine if this ratio needs adjustment, as well as ensuring all birds are healthy and free from disease.

Setting Up For Incubation

Setting up for incubation begins with selecting the right eggs and preparing the incubation environment.

Choose clean, uncracked eggs that have been laid within the last seven days for the best hatch rates. Store these eggs at a consistent temperature of around 55°F (13°C) and a humidity level of 70-80% until you're ready to incubate.

An incubator is essential for hatching eggs if you don't have a broody hen. It needs to maintain a stable temperature of 99.5°F (37.5°C) and a humidity level of around 50-55% for the first 18 days, increasing to 65-70% for the final three days before hatching. Place the incubator in a room with a stable environment, away from direct sunlight or drafts that could cause temperature fluctuations.

Ensure the incubator is clean and sanitized before use. Place the eggs with the pointed end facing down or horizontally if your incubator turns the eggs. Turning the eggs regularly, about three to five times a day, is crucial during the first 18 days to prevent the embryo from sticking to the shell.

Many modern incubators have automatic turners, making this process easier.

Incubation Techniques And Equipment

Several incubation techniques can be employed depending on your resources and preferences. The most common method is using a forced-air incubator, which circulates air evenly, ensuring a consistent temperature and humidity level. Still-air incubators, which don't circulate air, require careful monitoring to maintain the correct temperature gradients.

Equipment needed includes the incubator itself, a reliable thermometer, and a hygrometer to monitor humidity levels. Candling tools are also useful for checking egg fertility and embryo development. Candling involves shining a bright light through the egg to observe the contents.

This should be done at least twice during incubation—around day 7 and day 14—to remove any non-developing eggs that could spoil and contaminate the others.

Maintaining the correct humidity is crucial, particularly in the final days before hatching. Adding water to the incubator's reservoirs or placing damp sponges inside can help manage humidity levels. Ensure there's adequate ventilation in the incubator, as developing embryos need oxygen, especially as they grow larger.

Caring For Chicks After Hatching

Once the chicks hatch, they need a warm, safe environment. Transfer them to a brooder, which can be a simple box or commercial setup with heat, food, and water. The brooder temperature should be around 95°F (35°C) for the first week, decreasing by

5°F each week until they are fully feathered at around 6 weeks old.

Use a heat lamp or brooder plate to provide warmth, placing it so chicks can move away if they get too hot. Line the brooder floor with absorbent bedding like wood shavings, but avoid slippery materials that can cause leg issues. Ensure the brooder is secure from drafts and predators.

Provide chick starter feed, which is specially formulated to meet their nutritional needs, and fresh water in shallow containers to prevent drowning. Clean the water containers daily and ensure the bedding stays dry to avoid health issues. Observe the chicks regularly for signs of illness or distress, ensuring they are active and eating well.

Managing Breeding Programs

Managing breeding programs involves selecting the best birds to produce healthy, productive offspring. Start by identifying desirable traits in your flock, such as good egg production, robust health, and favorable temperament. Record keeping is crucial, noting the lineage, performance, and health issues of each bird.

Selective breeding focuses on enhancing these traits over generations. Pair birds that exhibit desired characteristics and monitor their offspring. Cull birds that don't meet the standards to avoid passing on undesirable traits. This process requires patience and careful observation to achieve long-term improvements in your flock.

Genetic diversity is also important to avoid inbreeding, which can lead to health problems and reduced productivity.

Introducing new bloodlines periodically can help maintain a healthy, vigorous flock. Breeding programs should be adaptable, allowing for adjustments based on changing goals or environmental conditions.

CHAPTER EIGHT

Egg Production And Management Collecting And Storing Eggs

Proper Egg Collection Techniques

Collecting eggs efficiently and correctly is crucial for maintaining their quality and ensuring the health of your flock. The best time to collect eggs is early in the morning and then again in the late afternoon. This minimizes the time eggs spend in the coop, reducing the risk of contamination and breakage. To collect eggs, gently reach under the hens, being careful not to startle them. Use clean hands or gloves to avoid transferring dirt or bacteria to the eggs.

Storing Eggs Correctly
Once collected, eggs should be stored properly to maintain freshness. Store eggs in a cool, dry place, ideally at a temperature of around 55°F (13°C) and a

relative humidity of 70-80%. You can use a dedicated egg fridge or a cool room. Eggs should be stored with the pointed end down to keep the yolk centered and reduce the risk of the air cell moving, which can affect freshness. It's also helpful to label the eggs with the date of collection to ensure proper rotation.

Cleaning Eggs

If eggs are soiled, they should be cleaned before storage. Dry cleaning with a brush or abrasive pad is preferred to avoid removing the egg's natural protective coating. If wet cleaning is necessary, use water that is warmer than the egg to prevent bacteria from being drawn through the shell. Dry the eggs immediately and store them as soon as possible.

Managing Egg Quality And Size

Factors Affecting Egg Quality

Several factors impact egg quality, including the hen's diet, health, and environment. Providing a balanced diet rich in calcium and protein is essential. Ensure the hens have constant access to clean water and maintain a clean, stress-free environment to promote consistent egg production. Regularly inspect the hens for signs of illness or stress, as these can affect egg quality.

Controlling Egg Size

Egg size is influenced by the hen's breed, age, and nutrition. Younger hens typically lay smaller eggs, which increase in size as they mature. To manage egg size, ensure a balanced diet tailored to the specific needs of your hens.

Adjusting feed composition to include more protein and calcium can help increase egg size. Additionally, managing the light exposure in the henhouse can stimulate consistent laying and affect egg size.

Handling and Sorting Eggs

Handling eggs carefully during collection and storage is crucial to maintaining their quality. Sort eggs by size and quality before packaging them for sale or storage. Discard any cracked or unusually shaped eggs to maintain a high standard for your customers. Properly handling and sorting eggs also helps in monitoring the flock's health and nutritional needs.

Understanding Egg Laying Cycles

Natural Egg Laying Cycles

Hens typically begin laying eggs at around 18-20 weeks of age, and their egg production follows a natural cycle influenced by light exposure.

Hens are most productive in the spring and summer when daylight hours are longer. Egg production tends to decrease during the fall and winter. Understanding these cycles can help you plan for seasonal variations in egg availability.

Managing Light Exposure

Artificial lighting can be used to extend daylight hours during shorter days, helping to maintain consistent egg production. Provide 14-16 hours of light per day by using timers to turn lights on before sunrise and off after sunset. This mimics the natural increase in daylight during spring and summer, encouraging hens to lay eggs consistently throughout the year.

Molting and Egg Production

Hens naturally molt once a year, typically in the fall, which can temporarily reduce or stop egg production. Molting allows hens to shed old feathers and grow new ones, and it usually lasts several weeks. During this period, it's essential to provide a high-protein diet to support feather regrowth and prepare the hens for the next laying cycle.

Troubleshooting Egg Production Issues

Common Production Problems

Several issues can affect egg production, including poor nutrition, stress, disease, and environmental factors. If egg production drops suddenly, evaluate the hens' diet to ensure it's balanced and meets their nutritional needs. Check for signs of stress, such as changes in behavior or feather pecking, and address any potential causes.

Disease and Parasite Control

Regular health checks and preventive measures are crucial to maintaining a healthy flock. Vaccinations, deworming, and parasite control can prevent diseases that impact egg production. If you notice any signs of illness, such as lethargy, reduced appetite, or abnormal droppings, consult a veterinarian for a proper diagnosis and treatment plan.

Environmental Adjustments

Ensure the henhouse is clean, dry, and well-ventilated to promote a healthy environment for your hens. Providing enough space and nesting boxes can reduce stress and encourage regular laying. Adjusting the temperature and lighting can also help maintain optimal egg production conditions.

Marketing And Selling Eggs

Creating a Marketing Plan

Marketing your eggs effectively involves understanding your target market and developing a strategy to reach them. Identify potential customers, such as local grocery stores, farmers' markets, and individual consumers. Use social media and local advertising to promote your eggs and highlight their quality, freshness, and any unique selling points, such as organic or free-range production.

Packaging and Presentation

Attractive and functional packaging can make a significant difference in how your eggs are perceived by customers. Use clean, sturdy cartons and label them with your farm's name, contact information, and the date the eggs were collected.

Consider adding information about your farming practices, such as free-range or organic, to appeal to health-conscious consumers.

Pricing and Distribution

Determine a competitive price for your eggs by researching local market prices and considering your production costs. Offer competitive pricing while ensuring you cover your costs and make a profit. Establish reliable distribution channels, whether through direct sales, local markets, or partnerships with retailers. Building strong relationships with your customers and distributors can help ensure consistent sales and growth for your egg production business.

CHAPTER NINE

Harvesting And Processing Meat

Best Practices For Slaughtering Chickens

Proper slaughtering practices are crucial for ensuring both the quality of meat and the welfare of the chickens. The first step is to ensure that the chickens are healthy and stress-free before slaughtering. Stress can negatively impact meat quality, so it's essential to handle the birds gently and keep them calm.

When preparing for slaughter, ensure that all equipment is clean and ready. This includes having a sharp knife or cleaver, a killing cone, and a scalding pot if you're doing traditional processing. The killing cone is used to hold the chicken securely while you cut. The bird should be positioned head-down in the cone, which helps to minimize stress and makes the process more efficient.

The actual slaughter involves making a swift and precise cut to the bird's jugular veins. This method allows for quick bleeding, which is essential for meat quality. The bird should then be hung to allow any remaining blood to drain completely. After this, the chicken is usually immersed in hot water (around 140°F or 60°C) for a few minutes to help loosen feathers, making plucking easier. Always follow local regulations and guidelines to ensure humane treatment and sanitary conditions.

Processing And Butchering Techniques

Once the chickens are slaughtered and properly bled, they need to be processed and butchered. The first step in processing is to remove the feathers, which can be done manually or using a feather plucker. Manual plucking involves pulling out feathers by hand, which is labor-intensive but effective for small-scale operations. For larger operations, a mechanical plucker can save time and effort.

After plucking, the next step is to eviscerate the chicken. This involves carefully removing the internal organs. To do this, make a small incision near the vent (the bird's rear opening) and gently pull out the intestines, liver, heart, and other internal organs. Be careful not to puncture the intestines, as this can contaminate the meat. Once the organs are removed, rinse the carcass thoroughly inside and out to ensure it's clean.

The final butchering step involves cutting the chicken into desired parts. The most common cuts include breasts, thighs, drumsticks, and wings. Use a sharp knife or poultry shears for precision. If you're unfamiliar with the best cutting techniques, consider watching instructional videos or practicing on a few birds to gain confidence.

Storing And Preserving Meat

Proper storage and preservation are essential for maintaining meat quality and safety. After butchering, the chicken should be immediately chilled to prevent bacterial growth. This can be done by placing the meat in a refrigerator or a cooler set to a temperature below 40°F (4°C). For long-term storage, freezing is the best option.

To freeze chicken, wrap each piece tightly in plastic wrap or aluminum foil, and place it in an airtight freezer bag. This helps to prevent freezer burn and preserve the meat's flavor and texture. Label each package with the date of freezing to keep track of its freshness. For best quality, use frozen chicken within 9 to 12 months.

If you prefer to keep the chicken for a shorter period, you can also opt for canning. This involves cooking the chicken in jars under high pressure to kill bacteria and seal the jars. Ensure you follow a reliable canning guide and adhere to safety standards to prevent contamination and spoilage.

Ensuring Meat Quality And Safety

Maintaining high standards of meat quality and safety involves several key practices. First, ensure that all equipment and surfaces used for processing are thoroughly cleaned and sanitized before and after each use. This prevents cross-contamination and helps to maintain a hygienic environment.

Next, monitor the temperature of your storage facilities. Meat should be kept at or below 40°F (4°C) in the refrigerator and 0°F (-18°C) in the freezer to prevent spoilage.

Always check the condition of the meat before use; any signs of discoloration, off smells, or slimy texture indicate spoilage.

Additionally, proper handling during processing is crucial. Always use gloves and clean tools to avoid direct contact with raw meat and reduce the risk of contamination. Following these guidelines ensures that the meat remains safe for consumption and retains its quality from slaughter to the table.

Marketing And Selling Poultry Products

Once the meat is processed and prepared, the next step is marketing and selling your poultry products. Start by identifying your target market, whether it's local restaurants, farmers' markets, or direct-to-consumer sales. Understanding your audience helps tailor your marketing strategy effectively.

Creating appealing packaging and labeling is important for attracting customers. Use clear, attractive labels that provide essential information, such as the product name, weight, and any certifications (e.g., organic or free-range). Effective branding can also help differentiate your products from competitors.

Consider leveraging social media and online platforms to reach a broader audience. Share engaging content about your farming practices, the quality of your products, and any special offers. Building a strong online presence can help increase visibility and attract new customers. Additionally, forming partnerships with local businesses and participating in community events can boost your market presence and sales.

CHAPTER TEN

Troubleshooting And Problem-Solving

Common Problems And Solutions

Chicken farming, like any agricultural venture, comes with its own set of challenges. Understanding common problems and their solutions can make the process smoother and more rewarding. One of the most frequent issues is disease outbreaks. Chickens are susceptible to a variety of illnesses, including avian influenza, Marek's disease, and coccidiosis. To prevent these, maintain a clean coop, provide proper ventilation, and ensure vaccinations are up-to-date. If an outbreak occurs, isolate the infected birds immediately and consult a veterinarian for appropriate treatment.

Another common problem is poor egg production. This can result from stress, inadequate nutrition, or improper lighting. Ensure your chickens have a balanced diet rich in calcium and protein. Provide at least 14 hours of light daily, especially during shorter winter days, to stimulate egg laying. If stress is the issue, create a calm environment by minimizing loud noises and handling the birds gently.

Feather pecking and cannibalism can also pose significant problems. These behaviors often arise from overcrowding, boredom, or nutritional deficiencies. Ensure your chickens have enough space—at least 2 to 3 square feet per bird inside the coop and 8 to 10 square feet per bird in the run. Provide enrichment activities such as perches, dust baths, and toys to keep them engaged. Check their diet to make sure it includes all necessary nutrients, particularly protein.

Dealing With Predators And Pests

Predators and pests can wreak havoc on a chicken farm if not properly managed. Common predators include foxes, raccoons, hawks, and snakes. To protect your flock, build a secure coop with sturdy materials. Ensure there are no gaps or holes larger than half an inch, as many predators can squeeze through small spaces. Use hardware cloth rather than chicken wire, as it is more resistant to tearing. Cover the run with a secure roof or netting to protect against aerial predators.

Regularly check for signs of digging around the coop, as some predators like foxes and raccoons will try to burrow underneath. Installing an apron of hardware cloth around the perimeter of the coop can deter these digging attempts. Additionally, consider using motion-activated lights or alarms to scare away nocturnal predators.

Pests such as mites, lice, and rodents can also cause problems for your chickens. Regularly inspect your birds for signs of mites and lice, such as excessive scratching or feather loss. Treat infestations promptly with appropriate insecticides and clean the coop thoroughly. To control rodents, keep feed in sealed containers and remove any spilled feed promptly. Setting traps and maintaining a tidy environment can help prevent rodent infestations.

Managing Unexpected Expenses

Unexpected expenses are an inevitable part of chicken farming. These can include veterinary bills, repairs to the coop, or sudden increases in feed prices. To manage these expenses, it's important to have a contingency fund set aside. Aim to save at least 10% of your monthly farm income for emergencies.

Buying in bulk can also help reduce costs. Purchase feed, bedding, and other supplies in larger quantities to take advantage of discounts. Establish a good relationship with local suppliers who might offer better prices or payment terms for regular customers. Additionally, consider growing some of your feed ingredients, such as corn or greens, to reduce reliance on purchased feed.

Regular maintenance of your coop and equipment can prevent costly repairs. Inspect the coop and run weekly for any signs of wear or damage, and fix small issues before they become major problems. Keeping detailed records of expenses and income can also help you identify areas where you can cut costs or improve efficiency.

Handling Behavioral Issues

Behavioral issues such as aggression, bullying, and excessive noise can disrupt your flock and reduce productivity. To handle aggression, first identify the cause. Overcrowding, lack of resources, or introducing new birds can lead to fighting. Ensure your chickens have enough space, food, and water. When introducing new birds, do so gradually, allowing them to see each other through a barrier before fully integrating.

Bullying often occurs when one bird is weaker or different from the others. Separate the bullied bird temporarily to allow it to recover. Provide hiding spots and multiple feeding stations to reduce competition. If bullying persists, it may be necessary to rehome the aggressive bird.

Excessive noise can indicate stress or discomfort. Check for environmental factors such as predators, changes in the coop, or lack of food and water. Addressing these issues can help calm your flock. Providing enrichment activities and ensuring a comfortable living environment can also reduce stress-related behaviors.

Resources For Further Help And Information

When faced with challenges, having access to reliable resources can be invaluable. Local agricultural extension offices often offer free advice and support for chicken farmers. These offices can provide information on best practices, disease management, and local regulations.

Online forums and social media groups can also be great resources. Joining a community of chicken farmers allows you to share experiences, ask questions, and learn from others. Websites such as BackyardChickens.com offer extensive libraries of articles and user forums where you can find information on virtually every aspect of chicken farming.

Books and publications from reputable sources, such as university extension programs or experienced farmers, provide detailed and reliable information. Titles like "Storey's Guide to Raising Chickens" by Gail Damerow are comprehensive and highly regarded in the chicken farming community.

Lastly, establishing a relationship with a local veterinarian who specializes in poultry can provide you with expert advice and support. Regular health checks and prompt attention to any medical issues can prevent small problems from becoming major challenges.

Frequently Ask Questions And Answers

What are the basic requirements for starting a chicken farm?

To start a chicken farm, you need suitable land, a well-ventilated coop, feeding equipment, waterers, and a reliable source of quality chicks or hens. Additionally, you'll need a consistent feed supply and knowledge of poultry care.

What breed of chickens should I raise?

The choice depends on your goals. For egg production, popular breeds include Leghorns, Rhode Island Reds, and Sussex. For meat, consider Cornish Cross and Broilers. Dual-purpose breeds like Plymouth Rock and Australorp are good for both eggs and meat.

How much space do chickens need?

Chickens need about 2-3 square feet of indoor space and 8-10 square feet of outdoor space per bird. Overcrowding can lead to stress and health issues.

What do chickens eat?

Chickens eat a balanced diet of grains, protein, vitamins, and minerals. Commercial feed is commonly used, supplemented with kitchen scraps, fresh greens, and insects.

How often should I feed my chickens?

Chickens should have access to food at all times. Typically, you'll refill feeders once a day. Ensure they have fresh water daily as well.

How do I keep my chickens healthy?

Maintain a clean coop, provide a balanced diet, and ensure fresh water. Regularly check for signs of illness, vaccinate as recommended, and provide proper ventilation and predator protection.

How do I protect chickens from predators?

Use sturdy coops with secure doors and windows. Install fencing around the coop and run, and consider using electric fencing for added protection. Lock chickens in the coop at night.

How often do chickens lay eggs?

Hens usually start laying eggs at around 18-20 weeks of age and can lay one egg per day, depending on the breed and environmental conditions.

What is the ideal temperature for chickens?

Chickens are comfortable in temperatures between 55-75°F (13-24°C). Provide shade and ventilation in summer and insulation and heat lamps in winter.

How do I clean a chicken coop?

Remove droppings, old bedding, and uneaten food regularly. Clean and disinfect the coop at least once a month. Replace bedding and ensure good ventilation.

How can I tell if a chicken is sick?

Signs of illness include lethargy, loss of appetite, unusual droppings, respiratory issues, and decreased egg production. Isolate sick birds and consult a vet.

What are common diseases in chickens?

Common diseases include Marek's disease, Newcastle disease, coccidiosis, and avian influenza. Regular vaccination and good hygiene practices can help prevent these.

How do I introduce new chickens to my flock?

Quarantine new chickens for at least two weeks to prevent disease spread. Introduce them gradually by allowing visual and limited physical contact before fully integrating them.

How long do chickens live?

Chickens typically live 5-10 years, depending on breed and care. Production hens may have a shorter lifespan due to intensive laying.

Can chickens be raised in urban areas?

Yes, many urban areas allow backyard chickens. Check local regulations for zoning laws, maximum flock size, and coop requirements.

How do I handle chicken manure?

Chicken manure is high in nitrogen and can be composted for garden use. Ensure it is properly aged or composted to prevent burning plants.

What is the best bedding for chickens?

Common bedding materials include straw, wood shavings, and sand. Ensure bedding is dry, absorbent, and regularly changed to maintain hygiene.

How can I increase egg production?

Provide a balanced diet, clean water, and sufficient lighting (14-16 hours of light per day). Reduce stress by maintaining a clean, predator-free environment.

Can chickens fly?

Most chickens can fly short distances. To prevent them from escaping, trim their wings or use covered runs and high fences.

How do I care for baby chicks?

Keep chicks in a brooder with a heat lamp, maintaining a temperature of 95°F (35°C) in the first week, decreasing by 5°F each week. Provide chick starter feed, fresh water, and clean bedding.

These questions and answers should provide a good foundation for anyone interested in chicken farming.

CONCLUSION

Chicken farming has evolved significantly over the years, reflecting the dynamic interplay between technological advancements, sustainability practices, and consumer preferences. As we look to the future, the industry stands at a pivotal crossroads, with the potential to shape the global food supply in profound ways.

One of the most critical aspects of modern chicken farming is its commitment to sustainability. As environmental concerns grow, the industry is increasingly adopting practices that minimize ecological impact. Innovations such as precision farming, which uses technology to monitor and optimize farm conditions, are becoming standard. These practices not only improve efficiency but also reduce waste and resource consumption, aligning chicken farming with broader environmental goals.

Animal welfare is another area where significant strides have been made. The push for humane treatment of chickens has led to improvements in housing conditions, nutrition, and healthcare. The implementation of free-range and organic farming methods provides alternatives to conventional systems, offering consumers more ethical choices. This shift is not merely a response to consumer demand but also reflects a growing recognition of the intrinsic value of animal welfare in agricultural practices.

Economic considerations remain a driving force in the industry. Chicken farming is a vital component of the agricultural sector, providing livelihoods for millions worldwide. The sector's economic health is closely linked to its ability to innovate and adapt to changing market conditions. The development of new breeds that grow faster and are more resistant to diseases is one example of how scientific advancements are enhancing productivity and profitability.

However, challenges persist. Disease management continues to be a significant concern, with outbreaks posing risks to both animal and human health. The industry must remain vigilant, investing in biosecurity measures and research to mitigate these risks. Additionally, balancing the demands of a growing global population with the need for sustainable practices requires ongoing effort and innovation.

Consumer preferences are also shaping the future of chicken farming. There is a growing demand for transparency and traceability in food production. Consumers want to know where their food comes from and how it is produced. This trend is driving the adoption of blockchain technology and other systems that can provide verifiable information about the origins and journey of chicken products from farm to table.

In conclusion, the future of chicken farming is promising yet complex. The industry must navigate a landscape marked by technological innovation, sustainability imperatives, animal welfare considerations, economic pressures, and evolving consumer demands. By embracing these challenges and opportunities, chicken farming can continue to play a crucial role in feeding the world, contributing to economic stability, and promoting sustainable agricultural practices. The journey ahead is one of continual adaptation and improvement, ensuring that chicken farming remains a cornerstone of global food security and environmental stewardship.

THE END

www.ingramcontent.com/pod-product-compliance
Lightning Source LLC
Chambersburg PA
CBHW071834210526
45479CB00001B/136